The Healing of the Soul

D1319798

Bert Bauman

The Healing of the Soul

DIMENSION BOOKS
BETHANY FELLOWSHIP, INC.
Minneapolis, Minnesota

Healing of the Soul
by Bert Bauman

Library of Congress Catalog Number 75-5445

ISBN 0-87123-223-5

Scripture Quotations are from
the Revised Standard Version

DIMENSION BOOKS
Published by Bethany Fellowship, Inc.
6820 Auto Club Road
Minneapolis, Minnesota 55438

Printed in the United States of America

Preface

When I first became a Christian it seemed as if all the problems of mankind could be solved by the new birth. Certainly my own pressing concerns fell away when I found new life through Jesus Christ. A whole new world opened up to me. But as time went on, the Christian life lost much of its importance and reality. New problems were born for which no solutions were in view. Then I heard of the baptism with the Holy Spirit and I quickly entered in. Again the immediate problems melted away, and I had an unfailing answer for any defeated Christian. It was so simple: receive the Holy Spirit and everything will fall into place. And it really worked for a time—until I found born-again Christians who had received the baptism with the Holy Spirit but were disillusioned and defeated.

Evidently more was needed. It was then God began to teach me the things in this book. Simply defined, it is the walk of faith. Regardless of the level of experience in God, the walk of faith is basic and cannot be commuted. There is no once-and-for-all answer—no simple solution to life. God has not so ordained it.

I have often wished I had known these things early in my life. Much distress and heartache could have been avoided. I pray that you who read this book will be the richer for it and will be spared some of the confusion and trouble which so doggedly haunts the footsteps of mankind.

Bert Bauman

Healing of the Soul

Someone once said, "There is in the heart of every man a God-shaped vacuum, and no man is satisfied until God fills it." In the beginning God occupied a place in the spirit of man. God was as much a part of the original design of man as the arms and legs He fashioned for his body. This union was broken through Adam's fall into sin. Man became an incomplete being because God as a vital part of man was cut off. The careful balance in his complex design was destroyed.

Every man since that time has felt an emptiness deep within. Just as he feels incomplete with the loss of a limb so he feels incomplete without God. Something is missing! There remains a deep, insatiable restlessness that is constantly seeking

HEALING OF

FAITH . . . is to reckon, consider, or depend upon what God says over against previous knowledge, experience or feelings. This is done by choice of will; therefore everyone can believe. Faith is agreeing with God. Positive use of the will (relative to God's Word) is faith; negative use is unbelief. You have power to set the will either upon the truth or the lie.

THOUGHTS in your mind may originate from God, yourself or Satan. Those thoughts you allow to remain are the thoughts you choose to think.

The thoughts you allow become habits—that is, thought-patterns or ATTITUDES. In other words, the thoughts you think determine your character and personality.

TRUTH

WILL

LIE

THOUGHTS ▸ ATTITUDES

UNBELIEF . . . is believing a lie—that is, depending upon, reckoning upon or counting upon a lie as though it were true. Whether done in ignorance or by choice the results are destructive since this leads to thoughts and reasonings based upon false foundations.

After choosing to believe God in any specific conflict, guard your mind to permit only those thoughts compatible with your choice. Remember, the thoughts in your mind do not all come from you. Learn to be selective. The mind must be renewed.

ATTITUDE, like character, is not easily changed. Your attitude determines your emotional health. Since attitude is developed by thought, it can only be changed by changing thoughts. Whatever is true, just, honorable, pure, lovely, think on these things.

While the principles outlined above are helpful to any person who has emotional, physical, or mental problems, it would be futile to speak of soul healing in depth unless the spirit of that person has first been healed. The spirit of man is the essence of man, and any true healing must take place from the inside out. Of course, there is only one way to receive spiritual health and that

THE SOUL

EMOTIONS or "feelings" result from attitude. Emotions must be controlled at the source by choosing to think true thoughts. Feelings can be changed through faith.

BEHAVIOR or actions follow emotions or feelings. Any person is capable of any act when emotions are developed and circumstances are just right for the act.

LIFE is all that which has to do with the well-being of body, soul and spirit. Love, joy, peace, goodness, patience, self-control and physical health. A life based upon truth leads to LIFE—

LIFE

EMOTIONS ▸ BEHAVIOR

DEATH

As an emotional being, man tends to be led by his feelings, equating feelings with reality. But man was designed to be controlled by his will. What a man chooses to believe is what he really is. "You can't help how you feel" is not true.

It is impossible to change some bad behavior patterns without first correcting the "false-truth" from which the behavior springs. Consequently changed thoughts will lead to new attitudes and a correction of behavior.

DEATH is all that which destroys body, soul and spirit. All anxiety, fear, despair, nervousness and sickness is a form of death.

is through receiving life itself in the person of Jesus Christ. Most of a person's emotional problems dissolve when the spirit receives life through Christ; however, for the problems that persist among Christians an understanding of the principles outlined above will be most helpful.

fulfillment, so man wanders from one tempting promise of satisfaction to another but finds no peace. Thus by turning to "things" for help rather than to God, man breaks the first commandment in his desperate search for completion. Consequently more and more misery and heartache is added to the restlessness within.

In the process of breaking the first commandment the other nine are also broken as man turns to the forbidden substitutes. If the first commandment were truly kept, the other nine would never be broken. All sin ultimately finds its root in turning to other gods. "Thou shalt have no other gods before me" is the wise counsel from the God who created man and knows infallibly what will satisfy his deepest needs. The commandments were intended as guidelines to help man return to his God and so be made whole again. Life will never be satisfactory until first of all God is restored to His original abode in the spirit of man.

Unfortunately the inner restlessness is misinterpreted and misdirected by most of mankind. Satan whispers that this hunger is for success, wealth, family, house, popularity, fame, sex, food, or a myriad of other things. Man, responding to this lie, goes in futile pursuit of these things. But

Jesus warns: "A man's life does not consist in the abundance of the things he possesses."

Though man continues to search for satisfaction in following one desire after another, his heart is not content. It continues to clamor persistently for inner peace. This is an ageless cry—a universal need present in every human soul. As the history of man moves on to its final moment, this cry will become more and more fervent. Anxieties, tensions, fears, frustrations and restlessness will continue to grow and multiply within the human family in ever-increasing density until complete collapse and destruction become an inescapable reality.

But there is hope. God has promised through Jesus Christ to "shorten those days" so that complete destruction of the human race will be avoided. But there is also a present hope—not for the human race in mass, but for the individual. The future hope is for the race. The present hope is for the individual alone. This individual and personal hope comes through an individual —Jesus Christ. It is He who promises, "Peace I leave with you; my peace I give to you; not as the world gives do I give to you. Let not your hearts be troubled, neither let them be afraid" (John 14:27). The peace He promises is given to the individual through the working of God as He forms Jesus Christ in the soul of a man. Again Jesus promises, "I have said this to you, that in me you may have peace. In the world you have tribulation; but be of good cheer, I have overcome the world" (John 16:33). Jesus Christ *is* peace; therefore it is through His life brought to birth and manifestation within the soul that the soul comes to rest. Peter, we read in Acts 10:36, preached "good news of peace by Jesus Christ."

It is good news indeed that God in the person of Christ will again fill the vacuum in man's life and so restore the original sense of completeness lost with the fall into sin. Jesus alone is God's program for peace and restoration of the restless, churning soul. Peace in the individual soul is therefore possible even though the environment is unfriendly—"in the world you have tribulation."

The peace which is Jesus overcomes the world. Apart from the actual forming of the life and character of Jesus Christ in the individual soul there is no peace. Depth of peace is enjoyed in direct proportion to the purity of Christ's nature formed in the soul. The individual who is conformed to the image of Jesus is the image of peace. Obviously, this is a work of which God alone is capable. He alone can produce Jesus Christ. Jesus can be conceived only by the Holy Spirit. But He has pledged himself to do this work for any individual who will permit it. "For those whom he foreknew he also predestined to be conformed to the image of his Son, in order that he might be the first-born among many brethren" (Rom. 8:29).

Just as the beginning of physical life takes place in an instant of time, so the life of Christ or spiritual life comes into being instantly. Thus Jesus taught Nicodemus in John 3:6. However, it is most important to recognize that after this spiritual conception the forming of Christ in the soul is a process of growth. A new-born child is complete and healthy in its stage of development, but it is not yet a mature adult. The personality can always be in balance and harmony at any particular stage of its development as it grows into maturity. Just so peace can be enjoyed by the believer regardless of his maturity, so long as the life of Christ is permitted to develop according to God's plan.

Christian perfection is a term which must take into consideration the growth process of Jesus Christ within the individual personality of each believer. The Bible in many places makes reference to growing into Christ. This process can be resisted, retarded or stopped by the individual. God requires the cooperation of the individual even though it is His power and working which produces the life of peace. He ever respects the individual will and does not work against it. The cooperation He requires from man is essentially the exercise of faith and permission to do His work. Permission is given in the form of continual prayer in which the believer asks for deliverance from the various sins and failures which the Holy Spirit points out to him. Ephesians 3:17 gives us the very key to peace: "And that Christ may dwell in your hearts through faith. . . . "

As we continue to consider the subject of soul healing, we shall attempt to set forth some principles which we trust will be helpful as we seek to cooperate with God in His work to produce the very image of Jesus Christ in us.

Body, Soul, and Spirit

"May the God of peace himself sanctify you wholly; and may your spirit and soul and body be kept sound and blameless at the coming of our Lord Jesus Christ. He who calls you is faithful, and he will do it" (1 Thess. 5:23-24). Much of what we have to say here is beautifully summarized in this portion of scripture. In earlier paragraphs we said mankind is desperately seeking inner peace. Here we find God's very name is peace. The peace man seeks is in Him, "the God of peace." He brings it to man through a complete renewing—"sanctify you wholly"—in three areas of man's being: "May your spirit and soul and body be kept sound." It is not a product of our efforts or works, for "He will do it." Notice again the scripture speaks of God's work involving three distinct areas within a man.

We must examine this thought more carefully. Unless we have a minimum knowledge of how we are made, faith and understanding are greatly hindered concerning many of the glorious promises of God. It is especially important to realize the distinction between the soul and spirit. Often the terms soul and spirit are used interchangeably and this has led to a great deal of confusion and misunderstanding of God's working and promises. When the Scriptures seem to use these terms interchangeably, it must be understood that it is referring to the life principle of the body. Thus when speaking of life in the body, either term may properly be used. However, as we shall see, there is a clear distinction between them. Each word identifies a specific part of our being with distinct individual faculties just as the body has certain distinct functions and capabilities.

In Hebrews 4:12 this distinction is further emphasized: "For the word of God is living and active, sharper than any two-edged sword, piercing to the division of soul and spirit, of joints and marrow, and discerning the thoughts and intentions of the heart." Though joints and marrow and thoughts and intentions are very closely related, they are nevertheless distinct and we must therefore conclude that soul and spirit are also distinct from each other.

DIAGRAM "A"

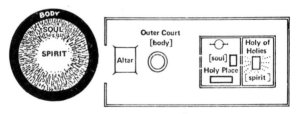

TABERNACLE

Diagram A will serve as an illustration of the three areas of our being. A similar illustration can be drawn from the design of the Old Testament tabernacle, which is a prefigure of the New Testament tabernacle; i.e., the born-again believer in whom the Holy Spirit dwells (1 Cor. 3:16-17). You will recall that the Old Testament tabernacle consisted of three areas: the outer court, the holy place, and the holy of holies. The holy place and the holy of holies though closely connected were two distinct areas and were enclosed by the outer court. It was in the innermost area, the holy of holies, that God took up His abode.

Just as the outer court enclosed the holy place and holy of holies, so the body of man contains his soul and spirit. Jesus Christ comes into and abides within the innermost being (spirit) of the believer just as God's glory rested in the holy of holies, the innermost part of the tabernacle. Without the indwelling Christ, the spirit of man is a darkened chamber. He is dead in trespasses and sins, separated from God with no real communication with Him. It is from within the "holy of holies" that God has always communed with man.

God meets man in the very essence of his being. The spirit is the true self—the eternal me. What a man is in the spirit is what he really is. God first enters into the eternal spirit of man, and from there He advances to the outermost of the person. It is in the spirit that God identifies and unites himself with man: "But he who is united to the Lord becomes one spirit with him" (1 Cor. 6:17). It is the spirit that gives life (soul) to the body. The spirit, the deepest part of man, may be compared to what psychologists name the unconscious self. The spirit merging or blending with the body produces the soul or conscious self. In other words, the soul is the conscious self—the conscious mind, will, and emotions. Whatever exists in the conscious self is a manifestation of the soul. Emotion, which is a faculty of soul, involves both tangible physical and intangible spiritual manifestations. For example, depression can be produced either by physical or mental causes. Hate, joy, love and fear involve the physical senses and frame as well as an incorporeal principle. Obviously, so do all our other conscious functions and emotions.

Since the soul owes its existence to the union of body and spirit, it no longer exists as the soul when this union is broken. At death a separation between body and spirit takes place. The spirit, together with that part of the spirit which was blended with the flesh forming the soul, returns to God and the body remains on the earth, lifeless. "The body without the spirit is dead"

(James 2:26). The following object lesson will crudely illustrate the relationship between body, soul and spirit. Take two rectangular pieces of glass or transparent plastic, one yellow and one blue. Let the yellow represent the spirit and the blue, the body. Now as you hold them to the light, slide them together so they overlap each other by one half. Observe the visual effect. Instead of two colors as you had originally, you now have three—yellow, blue, and green. The green owes its existence to the blue and yellow and does not exist when the two basic colors are separated. The green of course represents the soul. The soul, or conscious life of the body, owes its existence to the union of blue and yellow in our illustration. To state it simply: the spirit is the unconscious life principle, while the soul is the conscious life principle.

God's Three-Part Redemption

God is at work in three distinct areas of our being as He works out our redemption and restoration. This work He accomplishes through three different workings in three different periods of time—past, present and future. It is important that we understand the time element involved as well as the three parts of our personality. The spirit *has been* redeemed (a past work, 2 Cor. 5:17, Col. 3:1-4). The body *shall be* redeemed (a future work, Rom. 8:23, 1 Cor. 15:51). The soul is *now* in the process of redemption (a present work, Rom. 12:2, Eph. 4:17-23).

The redemption and restoration of the *whole* man is God's eternal purpose. He begins this in the heart of a man (the unconscious) by forming Christ in the spirit first of all. Then that spirit which has thus been made alive by reason of union with Christ is loosed into the soul (the emotions, feelings, thoughts, mind and choices of the will—that is, the conscious self). And finally that Spirit within will also make alive the physical body (the sensual self). God always works from the inside out, from the root to the top, from the seed to the flower, from the hidden to the manifest, from the spirit to the body.

It is essential that we understand the three time factors of God's working so that we may more fully cooperate with Him and avoid confusing and frustrating our faith in His promises. Let it be established first of all that when an individual receives Christ into his heart, He does come in (Rev. 3:20). He comes in to stay, for He says He will never leave us nor forsake us (Heb. 13:5). This is an operation of God in the spirit—the unconscious. He brings Christ to birth there as I open myself to Him and receive Him. I must simply believe and reckon upon God's word that He has taken up residence as He has promised since God does His work in the depth of my being (the spirit). This means I cannot feel what He does since it is below my conscious level.

We are told our personality is like a pyramid with only the top 10 percent peak representing our conscious self. The greatest part of my being lies below my conscious level. It is in this deepest part of me, my spirit or heart—not the body or soul—that God begins His life in me. Thus it becomes clear why we are asked to walk by faith. I simply have to count upon God's word as fact when He says He has done something in the depths of the 90 percent of my being that I am not conscious of. God knows more about the depths of my being than I do, and therefore His word is more reliable and true than my conscious feelings or knowledge.

This is a completed work that God does once and for all. It is God's *past* work. Henceforth I need only to count upon it to benefit from it. This is the foundation for the entire work of the redemption of the whole person. "Therefore, if any one is in Christ he is a new creation" (2 Cor. 5:17).

The future work of God, which is the redemption of the body, we shall not consider any further since it is a sovereign act of God's power which He shall bring to pass in the "twinkling of an eye" (1 Cor. 15:51-57; 1 Thess. 4:13-18).

The present work of God, which is the restoration of the soul, is the part of our redemption with which we are most concerned now. How to release the life which has been brought to birth in the unconscious realms of our being into the conscious daily experience is the problem which leads us into the warfare between flesh and spirit.

The battleground of this warfare is the area of the soul, or the conscious mind of man. The battlefield is not the spirit of the man as is so commonly accepted. Rather it is in the feelings, emotions, ideas, thoughts, conscious choices, decisions, and actions of the will that the battle rages. Man determines whether the principle of life in Christ or the principle of death will operate in his soul. Since the soul is made up of spirit and body, we find the pull of both to be present there. We find the pull of that which has been made new through Christ (the spirit) and that which has not yet been made new (the body). The principle of death resides in the members, while the principle of life resides in the spirit as we read in Romans 7. We are very conscious of the downward pull of sin but also of the upward pull to holiness and purity which originates from the life of Christ in the spirit.

Clearly, however, this conflict is in the soul, not in the spirit of the Christian. It is the soul which is split into two pulls, or natures, not the spirit. What I truly am—the eternal me—is a new creation (2 Cor. 5:17) united and made alive with Christ (1 Cor. 6:17). The old self has been put to death and buried (Rom. 6:3-11). Christ now is my true life (Col. 3:1-4). As He is, so are we in this present world (1 John 3:17). We are complete in Him (Col. 2:9-10). When He appears we shall be like Him (1 John 3:2). When the veil of the flesh is laid aside it will all be evident, but now we must walk by faith. In the spirit, we are not two natures but one new man—a united, purified, redeemed, new creation through the indwelling Christ. "I have been crucified with Christ; it is no longer I who live, but Christ who lives in me; and the life I now live in the flesh I live by faith in the Son of God, who loved me and gave himself for me" (Gal. 2:20). Those who are spiritually dead are dead in trespasses and sins and there can be no real or serious conflict. It is only as the life of Christ is born in a man's spirit that a conflict begins in dead earnest. The flesh wars against the spirit and the spirit against the flesh.

Where is the soul in this conflict? It is the prize of the conflict. To the winner go the spoils (Gal. 5:16-25). The soul will manifest that which I believe in. If I walk after the spirit—that is, believe and count on the truth of God concerning what I truly am in the spirit by virtue of the indwelling Christ—the flesh will not rule in my soul, but if I believe my senses and feelings over the Word of God and walk after them, my soul will manifest the works of the flesh. When the Scripture speaks of the flesh it includes that part of the soul which is flesh-oriented and Satan-taught. All we learn and know by nature ultimately turns inward toward self and sensuality. Thus even that which is "natural" in the world is fleshly and tainted and cannot be used by God. Only that which comes from the new creation is acceptable to God.

It is unquestionably the will of God to form the life of Christ in the soul of the believer; however, since God does not overrule the will of man, there is a part man must play in bringing this life into the emotions. Man's part is the positive exercise of the will upon the Word of God in a living, aggressive faith. Nothing less than this kind of faith, correctly understood and exercised, can be effective in this mighty battle to win the soul. Unbelief, ignorance and deception form a prison for the life of Christ, keeping Him locked within the spirit of man so that He cannot be released into the soul (conscious experience).

The condition of the soul is expressed through the actions and expressions of the body. The more spiritual the soul of a converted man is, the more of the virtues of Christ are displayed to the eyes and ears of the world. Faith releases the life of Christ into the soul. He permeates the consciousness of the believer and finally manifests Himself through the body to the world. The world cannot see Christ in a believer unless His life functions in the soul (the emotions, mind and will) which is in turn manifested through the body. It is impossible for the world to look upon a sad, discouraged countenance and see the life of Jesus.

A very dear friend of mine has been a Christian from his youth. I remember my first impression of him as a grouchy looking man with the corners of his mouth fixed in a perpetual downward curve. His countenance was no testimony to the grace of God in his heart. But a miracle took place in his life as he sat under the Word of Life. One evening as we sat in a meeting,

I was suddenly struck by the change in his appearance. A miracle had quietly occurred before my eyes and I only just then noticed it! His face was radiant with peace and joy and the corners of his mouth were turned upward instead of down. This has since been his natural expression, and people who meet him now see him as a man from whom love and joy seem to flow. What caused such a change even though he had been a Christian for many years? Simply, the life of Jesus, which had always been within him, was released as he received in faith the Word of God. I don't know at what moment the visible transformation took place. I only know that one day I suddenly saw Jesus in his face!

The manifestation of Jesus alone will draw men. He must be seen in the twinkle of an eye, which is the outward manifestation of a cheerful and joyful soul, or in the tear that overflows the eye from a soul moved with the compassion of Christ. But self-effort cannot produce Christ in the soul. Only faith can release His life into the soul. "But my righteous one shall live by faith" (Heb. 10:38).

The Power of the Lie

In the first chapter of Romans, God briefly summarizes the sinful condition of man and how he got that way. After turning away from God "they became futile in their thinking and their senseless minds were darkened." The beginning of a sinful life is a darkened mind. How does a mind become darkened? In Romans 1:25 we find the answer ".... because they exchanged the truth about God for a lie."

Just as God is the source of His word which is truth, so there is a personality behind the lie. The lie is the word of someone which is spoken contrary to the word of God. Jesus said that "someone" is Satan, the father of lies (John 8:44). The sad state of the human race all began with a lie. "You will not die," said the serpent. God's words were still fresh in Eve's ear, "You shall not eat of the fruit of the tree which is in the midst of the garden, neither shall you touch it, lest you die." She had two testimonies to count upon. One was the opposite of the other; both could not be true. She chose the wrong one—she believed a lie and acted upon what she believed. This unfortunate choice produced its fruit in her life, and all of her subsequent problems came as a result of counting upon that lie. This strategy was perfect and Satan has never changed it.

Every problem within you has its source in a lie from the father of lies. That is why there is only one way out and that is by faith —that is, believing the truth. Works of righteousness or sacrifice will not clear up a problem so long as one holds to the lie. No amount of prayer or penance will bring victory so long as one continues to depend upon any testimony which is contrary to the Word of God. When a lie is held in the mind long enough the truth does not seem right.

I once talked with a person who was a backslidden Christian. For years she wandered in the wilderness of sin. When she came to me, I told her again the simple story of the forgiveness of sin which she, of course, once knew very well. Her response to this very elementary gospel message was one of disbelief that God would not punish her for her past sins. She thanked me for my good intentions but apologetically explained that she felt I was propagating some new and strange doctrine. It was only after repeated teaching of the truth that the light of God's word finally penetrated the darkness of the lie and she was able to accept the forgiveness God offered her.

On one occasion I attended a function in an unfamiliar part of the city. Upon leaving the building, I got into my car and proceeded to take a street which I supposed would take me home. I was certain I was going in the right direction, even though after driving some distance no familiar landmarks appeared. I glanced at the auto compass. It indicated I was heading in exactly the opposite direction I wanted to go. I felt so right about the direction I was taking, however, that my first thought was that the compass had failed. I continued on for some distance grumbling to myself about the inaccuracy of the compass. Finally, however, when it became obvious I had lost my way, I decided to try believing the compass even though my feelings were completely contrary. I turned the car around and headed in the opposite direction. Of course the compass proved to be more reliable than my misguided feelings. For some time, though, the truth did not seem right, but as I continued to trust the compass, familiar sights began to appear and my feelings gradually changed to accept the veracity of the compass. The thoughts and feelings I entertained were all wrong because I had accepted a lie. I believed I was going north when in reality the direction was south.

The Word of God is our compass in life. It does not always feel right, but it will prove to be right if we act upon it. The very instant I turn from the false to the true, the bonds formed by the lie are broken. It is the very nature of light to dispel darkness, and likewise it is the very nature of truth to dispel the lie. The strength of a lie, however, is in our inability to recognize it. No one deliberately believes and depends upon that which is not real and true. Those who believe a lie are firmly convinced that what they are believing is the truth. In effect the lie is a "wrong truth"; that is, it has the appearance of truth to those who are deceived.

Deep within the thought patterns and attitudes of every human there are countless hidden lies. The thoughts we think naturally fall along the paths of the truths or lies we receive into our minds. Whenever a lie is introduced and kept in the personality, it becomes the foundation and seed for thought patterns which have their roots in that lie. These satanic seeds are continually growing and bringing forth their destructive fruits in the personality. It is these hidden lies that are the most dangerous because they have found their way into the heart without challenge or examination. We assimilate most of these lies from the world around us. The whole world is in the power of the wicked one. Even parents, teachers and best friends often plant satanic seeds in our souls. The impressionable souls of children are especially sinned against. The soul that came so clean and untainted from the hand of God is soon perverted and twisted into the likeness of the fallen race instead of the likeness of God as He intended.

Much of what we are today is the result of that which we have accepted as truth in the years past. Few of us know what our true personality is. We are a mixture of the original true personality and that which has been disrupted and twisted by the fears, defenses and anxieties resulting from the lies and manifold workings of satanic forces.

We meet a person and are pleased or displeased with his personality. We say he has a timid, fearful, quick-tempered, evil, lustful or what-have-you type of personality. What we really see is a perverted image of what God originally intended. Often the thing we despise most in an acquaintance is the twisted remnant of his finest virtue. It is the wonderful plan and purpose of God to correct and restore this twisted personality to the glorious creation He originally intended it to be. This He does through Jesus Christ who is the firstborn among many brethren. We shall be like Him —a pure creation of God. This does not mean an exchange of personality but rather a *purifying* of personality.

The essential nature of Jesus is purity. This purity sets the original creation free so it is the true original creation of God that is manifested through the believer. It is interesting to note the various personality differences of the various authors coming through in the writings of the Bible, and yet the entire Scriptures breathe the purity of God's truth. God does not overrule and submerge the human personality, but rather lifts, inspires, frees and purifies it. We become like Him in the essential nature of His being, but each individual remains an individual and not a rubber-stamp duplication. The very creation itself reveals this wisdom of God in the infinite variety of every snowflake, flower or blade of grass.

The promise of God to the believer is that every part of his personality will be brought into proper balance. Each emotion is to be purified and functioning in the way and degree God originally intended. All perversion will be corrected. To accomplish this miracle, however, God wants my full cooperation. More than that, He wants me to work out what He has put within, and that is Christ himself. This pure Christ is released into my personality through the power of faith—faith in God and the truth as it is revealed in the Bible.

The Renewing of the Mind

In the process of being conformed to Christ in the area of the soul, the key is the attitude of the mind. The ideas, philosophies, thought patterns and memories that prevail in the mind form the outward conduct. These things control the emotions and cause one to be the particular person he is, at least to the outward observer.

Before a man becomes a disciple of Christ, he acts, thinks, talks and behaves like the rest of the world because he has been trained by the world. The world has been trained by the prince of this world and is therefore essentially under the control of his spirit (1 John 5:19). After a man's *spirit* is changed (converted) through the indwelling Christ, his *soul* is essentially what it was before conversion because he still has most of the old thoughts and habits in his mind. The new life principle, however, immediately begins to work and the Holy Spirit begins to enlighten the darkened areas with the truth of God's Word. The teachings of Jesus begin to penetrate the network of false teaching and ideas which have accumulated in the mind and the believer begins to act differently—he begins to resemble Jesus in his conduct. Jesus Christ, who is the truth, is formed in the soul whenever a lie is rejected in favor of the truth. "If you continue in my word, you are truly my disciples, and you will know the truth, and the truth will make you free" (John 8:31-32). "So if the Son makes you free, you will be free indeed" (John 8:36).

From these words of Christ it is again apparent that if the truth will free, the basis of the bondage must obviously be a lie. A lie is a wrong thought or idea that is held in the mind; hence a vital part of God's work in us is to renew the mind. Romans 12:2 indicates that transformation from the old ways of life to the new life in Christ takes place through the renewal of the mind: "Do not be conformed to this world but be transformed by the renewal of your mind, that you may prove what is the will of God, what is good and acceptable and perfect." Again in Ephesians 4:23 we read, "and be renewed in the spirit of your minds, and put on the new nature, created after the likeness of God in true righteousness and holiness." Verse 22 of this chapter shows us that the old ways which belong to the former manner of life are corrupt through *deceitful* lusts. Sinful living is the result of deceit, and so we read in verse 23 that the way to put off these old ways which have become our manner of living through deceitful lusts is to have the mind renewed into the truth as it is in Jesus (vv. 20-21). The renewing of the mind puts off the old and puts on the new: "Therefore, putting away falsehood, let every one speak the truth" (v. 25).

Krisy* was a personable and talented young girl. Because of her musical ability she was much sought after by the churches in her city. Though she had accepted Christ and recieved the baptism with the Holy Spirit as a teenager, she nevertheless fell into homosexual bondage early in life. Consequently she was rejected by church after church and she reacted with open rebellion. The first time I saw Krisy was in a small home meeting in which I was teaching. She sat slouched in her chair with arms folded, peering out from under sullen eyebrows. However, her unhappy heart drove her to seek counseling help.

Like most homosexuals, Krisy blamed her unhappy life on a narrow-minded society that would not accept homosexuals. When I suggested that sin causes unhappiness and that the real cause of her misery was her homosexual practice, she could not agree. She reasoned that showing love for another human being could not be wrong and therefore she would not accept the

---

* Krisy is a fictitious name, but the account is true.

scriptures which pointed to homosexuality as sin.

It was only after months of accepting her as she was and the patient teaching of God's Word that Satan's lie to her was broken. She made a decision to submit to God by receiving His word. One day she deliberately chose to count her homosexual life as sin because God said it was and for no other reason. Her feelings and reasonings had not changed, but she made a willful choice over her own ideas to trust and believe God's word. From that day on, a noticeable change came into her life. The rebellious spirit was broken and her personality began to normalize.

The life of Christ within her triumphed and today she is happily married with two children. Her love for Jesus is demonstrated in her concern for others in need.

If you will be free from the bondages and effects of sin you must become a lover of the truth. You must seek the truth and follow after it with all your heart. Nothing must be allowed to stand which is not true, regardless of how convincing or comfortable it may seem. Truth is the only foundation worth building your life upon. The teachings of Jesus Christ form the foundation of a happy, worthwhile life. You must

be convinced of that and allow the H
Spirit to reveal every thought and convic-
tion in you that is contrary to Christ's teaching and life. You must have your mind completely renovated so that Christ's teachings
and thoughts are your thoughts and philosophies. It is out of this storehouse that we
act and feel, for as a man thinks in his
heart so he is. You must bring every
thought into the captivity of Christ (2 Cor.
10:5). And let His mind dwell in you (Phil.
2:5). The believer who builds his life on
Christ's teaching is a wise man, and he
who does not is a foolish man (Matt. 7:24).
One holds to the truth, the other to a lie.
Only reality is worth building upon, and
the teachings of Jesus are reality.

Demons and "The Lie"

It is sometimes necessary in the case
of severe bondage to enlist the aid of another Christian. "Therefore confess your
sins to one another, and pray for one another, that you may be healed. The prayer
of a righteous man has great power in its
effects" (James 5:16).

Often a lie has become so entrenched
and the personality so deeply bound by it
that the individual seems powerless to

break free by himself. For such times God has given fellow Christians so that the available power may be multiplied: "And though a man might prevail against one who is alone, two will withstand him. A threefold cord is not quickly broken" (Eccles. 4:12). There is great spiritual strength where two or more Christians combine their faith and power in total unity against the enemy: "Truly, I say to you, whatever you bind on earth shall be bound in heaven, and whatever you loose on earth shall be loosed in heaven. Again I say to you, if two of you agree on earth about anything they ask, it will be done for them by my Father in heaven. For where two or three are gathered in my name, there am I in the midst of them" (Matt. 18:18-20).

It is often necessary to bind the evil spirit behind the lie so the individual is free to believe the truth. A lie is a false idea and ideas are the product of intelligence; therefore, it is clearly an intelligent entity— a spirit—who introduces a lie into the mind. As the anti-Christian idea is accepted, the evil spirit gains ground to make his home in an area of the personality. This is commonly called "demon possession."

I am aware of the controversy whether or not Christians can be demon possessed, and most of it centers in personal opinions.

That which does not is, in my opinion, a matter of semantics. It has been my obvious experience in counseling and ministering to Christians in bondage that they are often under the control of an evil spirit. I do not believe, however, Christians can be possessed by demons in the same way as the unsaved. So-called "possession" in Christians is more a matter of yielding control of an area or areas of the body, emotions or mind. This control may be gained by the adversary through deception or temptation to sin. Or in some cases, control may have been gained in childhood through the sins and occult activity of the parents. No power of darkness may inhabit the heart or spirit of a born-again Christian since Jesus Christ lives there and darkness cannot be where there is light: "But he who is united to the Lord becomes one spirit with him" (1 Cor. 6:17).

As I said before, demons gain and hold control through deception, that is, by enticing the individual to believe and accept a lie as the truth. These demonic lies are often the cause of deep and serious afflictions to both emotions and body. A capable young girl of 25, with all of life before her, was obsessed by the lie that she would die before 30 years of age. This naturally caused a seriously unsettled state of mind, and harassing physical and emotional sensations followed. During the day she would experience burning feelings in her chest, and often at night she would awaken, choking and unable to breathe.

The lie which produced this helotry was cleverly planted through a series of experiences. She was in love with a young Christian man and as sometimes happens, they fell into an overly intimate relationship. Consequently, she came under heavy guilt feelings, so when her young man was unexpectedly taken with a terminal disease and died before his 30th birthday, she interpreted this as God's punishment for their misconduct.

Using the vehicles of guilt and condemnation, Satan was able to float his destructive lie into this girl's soul, persuading her to expect the judgment of God to fall upon her with the same sentence. Though she was usually a rational, self-reliant and confident person, she became firmly convinced that she would die by her 30th birthday, as her fiancé had.

Within a short time her personality began to disintegrate. She sought psychiatric help; however, because of her Christian views, the psychiatrist's counsel was unacceptable to her. Her medical doctor then put her in touch with our ministry. I remember the tension I felt coming from this troubled girl when we first met. We began to pray for her, and sometimes it was necessary to rebuke, in Jesus' name, the spirits behind her bondage. At the same time I led her to take hold of the word of God concerning forgiveness for her sins and to depend upon the strength of Jesus Christ who indwelt her. She had to learn to discount her wrong feelings and instead depend utterly upon the truths of God's word. This she began to do faithfully.

In order to know the truth, she determined to be present at every Bible study. This decision seemed simple enough but at first she endured a real struggle in fulfilling it. When the hour for meeting came she usually did not feel like going and was tempted to stay in the security of her room. Fortunately she responded to this temptation by resolving that the less she felt like attending the more she was determined to go. As she made these choices, God gave her strength to seek Him, and there were very few meetings she ever missed. As she conscientiously and devotedly built into her life the things she heard, healing came into her soul. The lies of Satan were broken and ultimately the harassing physical symptoms stopped. The will of God has become her goal in life, and many people have been helped through her since her healing.

It is necessary for troubled people to know what God says in His Word if they are ever to live normally. Much of the current emphasis on exorcism is lacking and fails to bring lasting help because of the failure to understand the part demonic lies have in possession. The truth of God is indispensable for permanent deliverance.

The Christian who learns to confess and count upon the facts of God's Word and who seeks to live in submission to God need never fear the possession or control of evil spirits. On the other hand, Satan and his emissaries are the enemies of the Christian, and he works through the world and the flesh to hinder, harass or control areas of the Christian's life by tempting him to live after the flesh and believe a lie. "For we are not contending against flesh and blood, but against the principalities, against the powers, against the world rulers of this present darkness, against the spiritual hosts of wickedness in the heavenly places. Therefore take the whole armor of God, that you may be able to withstand in the evil day, and having done all, to stand" (Eph. 6:12-13).

The first step to freedom, then, must be to recognize the lie and confess it as sin to God. Believing a lie is really the sin of unbelief, since it is the opposi... God says. When a person believes ... is really taking Satan's word over ... word. This is what the Bible calls unbe..., and it may be engaged in deliberately or in ignorance. Either way, the practical results are the same, and repentance is necessary for deliverance. "If we confess our sins, he is faithful and just, and will forgive our sins and cleanse us from all unrighteousness" (1 John 1:9).

When sin is confessed, the individual is renouncing the alliance with Satan and submitting to God. Satan's power is thus broken through the blood of Jesus Christ which *has already* purchased forgiveness of sins for everyone. Thank God for the forgiveness of *your* sin and then declare your independence from Satan through the blood of Jesus, taking back all ground you yielded to him by compromise. Speak the words aloud after this manner: "You deceiving spirit of (hate, lust, fear, etc.), I command you in the name of Jesus Christ to depart from me. I hereby resist you and renounce you with all of your thoughts and ideas and I take back all ground I have ever yielded to you. I belong to God through the blood of Jesus, and my body is the temple of the Holy Spirit. I choose to believe God and serve Him."

As you do this, know that the evil spirit's power over you is broken and he *must* leave you. You know this not necessarily because your feelings change but because God's Word tells you Satan must obey you in the name of Jesus, and he must therefore leave you. "Submit yourselves therefore to God. Resist the devil and he will flee from you" (James 4:7).

The evil spirit may persist, attempting to cause you to lose faith and yield to him again, but he *must* go if you remain steadfast in your believing God: "Be sober, be watchful. Your adversary the devil prowls around like a roaring lion, seeking someone to devour. Resist him, firm in your faith, knowing that the same experience of suffering is required of your brotherhood throughout the world" (1 Pet. 5:8-9). Remember, through your union with Jesus Christ you have the authority of His name and Satan must obey you. "Behold, I [Jesus] have given you authority to tread upon serpents and scorpions, and over all the power of the enemy; and nothing shall hurt you" (Luke 10:19). "And these signs will accompany those who believe: in my name they will cast out demons . . . " (Mark 16:17).

As you are resisting Satan in this way, it is vital that you turn from all known sin in your life. Make no excuses but bring it all before God. Two sins are especially important to deal with: (1) bearing a grudge (the unforgiving attitude), and (2) occult experimentation (astrology, Ouiji boards, seances, fortune-tellers, etc.), which is the sin of idolatry, the breaking of the first and great commandment: "Thou shalt have no other gods before me." When seeking these forbidden arts, you are actually asking for information and help from Satan's kingdom and therefore come under subjection to him. Obviously, you cannot cast out Satan on the one hand and invite him in with the other.

Satan's right to you is broken through receiving forgiveness of sin from God, and if we are to receive forgiveness for ourselves, we must forgive the sins of others. "For if you forgive men their trespasses, your heavenly Father also will forgive you; but if you do not forgive men their trespasses, neither will your Father forgive your trespasses" (Matt. 6:14-15). (See also Matt. 18:23-35.)

I believe these two sins are at the root of most emotional problems and spiritual bondages. Be sure you are clear in these areas! Turn from *all* occult investigation. Dispose of all articles and books connected with the occult that may be in your dwelling and formally renounce any past practices in the manner mentioned in a previous paragraph. Allow no resentment, bitterness, hard feelings, anger, hatred, grudge or ill will toward any human being in your heart. Ask the Holy Spirit to reveal any of these things in your life. Often grudges lie buried in the subconscious, lost to the conscious memory, but they nevertheless provide an open door for evil spirits to harass you.

It has been necessary to dwell upon these negative truths, but it is the positive truths of God which bring deliverance and healing. Do not allow yourself to become demon-centered, or become overly introspective. Having dealt with the devil, let your mind dwell on the good news in God's Word. Study your Bible, especially the New Testament. Learn to acknowledge and reckon upon your position in God through His mercy and grace. God has placed you into Jesus Christ and Christ in you! Stand there by faith. You *are* "far above all rule and authority and power and dominion" through Jesus Christ. (Read Ephesians 1:18-23.) "For in him the whole fulness of deity dwells bodily, and you have come to fulness of life in him, who is the head of all rule and authority" (Col. 2:9-10). Though you may be the poorest of Christians, because you are in Christ and have His name, you have been placed over Satan by God's supreme authority. Satan has no rightful power over you. He can only dominate you as you yield to him through compromise or believing his lies!

This brings us back to the principle of faith. No release is permanent if you do not believe God's Word. You may have demons cast out every day and still not be free if you continue to believe false information (which may be your feelings) rather than God. Victory is yours through the truth! Jesus said, "If you *continue in my word*, you are truly my disciples, and you will know the truth, and the truth will make you free" (John 8:31-32).

It may be helpful to understand Satan's methods to induce bondage by comparing him to a hypnotist. It is my opinion that this entire principle was taught to humans by deceiving spirits. A great deal of false doctrine and false religion has been produced through hypnosis. Satan is the first hypnotist. He brings individuals under his control through a form of hypnosis. In order to be hypnotized, one must agree with the hypnotist by accepting his suggestions as true even though the suggestion is false. One of the first suggestions made is, "You are getting sleepy." This is not true, but as the subject accepts the suggestion he begins to act as a very sleepy person and so, step by step, the hypnotist leads his subject into his control until the most ridiculous suggestions are accepted and acted out by the subject. If told he is a monkey, the subject will immediately act like one. Of course he does not become a monkey, nor will he ever be one, but he acts like one because he believes he is one.

In exactly this way Satan gains control. After coming under his hypnotic spell by accepting his lies, people (and often Christians) begin to act out the suggestions he gives them. These suggestions may come to them through their feelings, friends or any other agent. The effect will be a wrong idea in their mind which is contrary to God's truth.

Many Christians are tormented by the thoughts that they are some kind of perverse or evil thing. I have known sincere Christian people who somehow acquired a fear and suspicion of being homosexual, when in fact there was no real basis for the fear. It was an idea which was somehow planted in their minds and grew bigger in time. Such ideas may easily be translated into experience should circumstances be conducive. Such was the case with Krisy, whom we discussed earlier. A very essential part of her continued victory lay in her denying Satan's lie that she was homosexual and believing instead in Jesus Christ as her *true* life. Once she had repented of her sin, it was necessary for her to believe the word of God which declared the "old Krisy" dead and Jesus Christ as her new *real* self. Clearly then, since Jesus is obviously not homosexual, she could not be either. It is evident that this same word of truth applies to every Christian regardless of the particular sin or bondage.

Do not believe those witnesses which are contrary to God's Word. When you become a Christian, Jesus Christ becomes your life and you must begin to believe what He is in you and no longer confess what you were in the past or what your present feelings may be if contrary to what God's Word declares to you. Remember, Christ is within you. Do not come under Satan's hypnotic spell. The truth sets you free! Christ in you is the hope of glory!

How to Have Faith

The key to receiving help from God is faith. Everything I have said to this point is useless without faith. In one way or another I have made constant reference to this essential ingredient to soul healing.

When Christians are asked for a definition of faith, various confusing and nebulous answers are given. You have been called to "walk by faith"; therefore you must have a clear, meaningful understanding of this vital Christian virtue if you are to be successful in your quest for deliverance, victory and soul healing.

"And without faith it is impossible to please him" (Heb. 11:6). "But my righteous one shall live by faith, and if he shrinks back, my soul has no pleasure in him" (Heb. 10:38). "For we walk by faith, not by sight" (2 Cor. 5:7). "All things are possible to him who believes" (Mark 9:23).

So then, what is faith? How do I understand it? Is it a feeling, or a mental exercise? "I just can't believe," we often say. By this we mean, "It is not reasonable . . . I cannot accept it intellectually," or "I do not feel the emotion of confidence that this is true." In this subtle way feeling and reason make up our concept of faith. But is it possible for anything made up of these two ingredients to be called faith? If faith depended upon the intellect or reason, those with the highest IQ would be richest in faith.

No, faith cannot be either a feeling or a mental exercise since the Word of God often calls upon us to believe in spite of natural abilities or feelings. Faith cannot depend upon reason because reason is exercised upon the foundations of our experiences and knowledge (which is often inaccurate) and God presents promises which are beyond natural knowledge or experience. The promises of God are always impossible to the natural mind and therefore unreasonable. Likewise faith cannot depend in any way upon feeling—not even the feeling of confidence, which is basically an emotion and therefore subject to the instability of all human emotions. Confidence (or assurance) may be the *result* of faith but it is not faith itself!

The hopeless confession "I just can't believe," which is so common to our experience, is the result of our deluded concept of faith. We are deceived into thinking we have no control over our faith when, in reality, we do. We can believe! If it were true that man has no control over his faith, Jesus would not hold him responsible; but, in fact, the heaviest responsibility possible is put upon an individual to believe. His eternal destiny is at stake in his faith, for Jesus said, he that does not believe shall be damned.

What then is faith and how can I have it? In John 7:17 Jesus indicates that it all begins with the will. "If any man's will is to do his will, he shall know whether the teaching is from God or whether I am speaking on my own authority." According to this teaching, I must will to do the truth, and Jesus promises that if I set my will I shall know the truth. Now the will is a deliberate choice that is made apart from feelings or intellectual reason. We are not to be *ruled* by our emotions, ideas or thoughts. God has so made us that we are to be ruled by our choices—by the will.

However frail or infirm the beginning choices may be, the course of life will be changed. A dear middle-aged widow of a medical doctor came to me for help. She was emotionally devastated and had lost all hope in life. To go on seemed futile and purposeless to her and to make matters worse, she appeared to have been stripped of all faith. When I pointed her to Jesus, she could not believe He existed. When I quoted the Bible, she doubted that it was true. When I suggested she simply call upon God, she could not since she was uncertain that He was real. Clearly she needed God, but I could find no place at which to begin to help her. Eventually, however, I led her into making use of her will by making a simple choice. I suggested she choose God by praying this most elementary prayer, "God, if there is a God, help me. And Jesus, if you exist, please come into my life. As best I know how I choose you." Frankly, I held little hope for any immediate results from such feeble faith, but I was amazed to see that it was sufficient for her to find God! God became very real to her, and with renewed life she became a faithful disciple of Jesus Christ.

So faith begins with the will. Realizing that faith begins as a volitional act, it is apparent that God has given to every man the potential of faith. The positive use of the will, together with all the thought processes and attitudes which follow, we call faith. The negative use of the will, together with all the thought processes and attitudes which result, we call unbelief.

Faith and unbelief are the same power in action—the difference is simply the direction into which the power is channeled. This obviously makes unbelief as destructive as faith is constructive. This great power lies within every man and can be used either for or against himself. The essential difference between the atheist and the saint is in the use of the will. The saint at one time or another was plagued with similar thoughts and ideas as those which come to the athiest, but by setting his will against those thoughts and choosing instead the thoughts and ideas of God, his life is producing the fruits of faith, while the atheist reaps the harvest to which he has set his will.

In lesser degrees we are all constantly making similar choices. As every problem arises, we put this power within us into action, either constructively or destructively. We put our faith either in God or in the problem. Let me underscore this in your mind: it is the same force or power at work either for you or against yourself! It all depends upon your choice—your will. There is no difference in essence between faith and unbelief. They are twins born from the same womb but living opposite lives.

In the long journey from Egypt to Canaan, the children of Israel illustrated the truths God wants mankind to know. In Psalm 78 God reveals His displeasure with them because of certain failures on their part, for we read in verses 19 through 22: "They spoke against God saying, 'Can God spread a table in the wilderness? He smote the rock so that water gushed out and streams overflowed. Can he also give bread, or provide meat for his people?' Therefore, when the Lord heard, he was full of wrath; a fire was kindled against Jacob, his anger mounted against Israel; because they had no faith in God, and did not trust his saving power." Notice especially the last verse, in which the reason for God's displeasure is summarized. Two things are mentioned: "no faith in God" and "did not trust his power." In other words, they did not consider Him to be *faithful* or *able*. They were not sure He could do what He said, or if He could, they were not sure He could be trusted to do it. The author of Hebrews when referring to this wilderness experience uses the terms "rebellion," "hardening of heart," "evil, unbelieving hearts," "disobedience." All these terms suggest the use of will in deliberate opposition to God.

It is not by accident that the Holy Spirit holds up Abraham and Sarah as examples of faith. In Psalm 78 we found God's definition of unbelief: lack of faith (unbelief) is *considering* God to be *un*faithful and *un*-able. God gives us a positive definition of faith in exactly opposite terms in Romans 4:21 where we read that Abraham *considered* God to be *able* and in Hebrews 11:11 in which we read that Sarah considered God to be *faithful*. The Holy Spirit is therefore clearly teaching us with both negative and positive examples that faith is a deliberate choice of one's will to *count or reckon* upon God to be *faithful* and *able* to do what He has promised.

This choice of will is to be exercised in the face of the most convincing contrary evidence—even when that evidence is found in my own feelings or convictions. "Let God be true though every man be false" (Rom. 3:4). Indeed, from two passages in 1 John it is evident that if we receive any other testimony above the testimony of God, it is the same as calling Him a liar. Do we accept the testimony of our reason or feelings above that which God has declared? If so, we put our feelings and emotions above God and inadvertently call Him a liar. To call anyone a liar is to cast doubt upon the worthiness of his character. We cannot say we trust the character of a friend and at the same time say his word cannot be relied upon. Thus the respect with which we receive the word of a person reveals the measure of our judgment of his character. "Have faith in God," Jesus said. This trust in Him will be manifested in our lives by our believing and reckoning upon His Word.

Faith and Fact

Faith is only possible when resting upon a fact. It is not possible to believe something is true when in reality it is not. The Word of God is fact, and true faith is simply counting upon a fact. Faith does not *make* a fact true, but it depends and reckons upon a fact as *being* true. So often we hold the mistaken idea that we will make a word of God true by believing it. In other words, we try to believe something is true so that

it might truly be so. We try to bring
reality by believing it into existence
concrete reality of the truth, then, dep
upon my faith to create it. This makes faith
a work and my faith the center of attention.
No wonder we have trouble with faith! God
does not call upon us for such mental gym-
nastics. He simply asks us to count upon
a fact and what He has declared is fact
whether or not I believe it.

Faith which is conscious of itself is not
faith at all. Faith is conscious only of God
and His Word and therefore unconscious
of itself. Our attention must be focused
away from self-effort unto God and His
Word. Counting upon that which is real and
true brings us into the benefits of that fact.
Doubting its reality keeps us from depending upon it; therefore we do not inherit its
benefits. It is as though a rich man made
a deposit of $1,000 to the account of a pov-
erty stricken man, and then announced that
fact to him. If the poor man believes the
report and begins to count on the word of
the rich man, he will benefit from the rich
man's gift. If he does not believe or count
upon the good news, he could starve to
death even though the $1,000 is his in all
reality and fact. His believing the announcement does not make the rich man's gift
a fact (that is so, regardless), but his be-

lieving the rich man's word brings the benefit of the gift, because the poor man would
begin to use the money given to him.

So it is with the truth of God's Word:
I do not have to make it true by believing—it
is true already! It is, in fact, true whether
I believe it or not, but I do not benefit from
that which is true if I do not count upon
it. This is the foundation of all God's deal-
ings with mankind. "In the beginning was
the Word." The word of God always comes
first. He announces to us what He has
already done, and as I count upon His
announcement it is manifested to me according as I believe. There are three steps
in receiving from God: (1) God makes an
announcement (promise). (2) Man counts
it to be true and continues to count upon
it (faith and patience). (3) God manifests
His promise to me (possession).

Faith and the Will of God

If faith is the choice of my will to reckon
or depend upon a declaration of God, it obviously follows that I must have a clear
word to count upon. It is impossible to have
a clear faith without a clear word of God
to depend upon. In other words, I must be
absolutely clear as to the will of God in
a given matter if I am to have a clear,
unhindered faith. The Word of God reveals

the will of God. If I can find a promise in the Bible which directly applies to my need or a general promise which may be applied in principle, I have a solid foundation upon which to base my faith. Any so-called faith exercised when the will of God is uncertain is only wishful thinking or self-delusion. God warns, "You ask and do not receive, because you ask wrongly, to spend it on your passions" (James 4:3).

I cannot seriously believe God will do something if there is any doubt that He wants to do it. Thus the first and most important ingredient in the faith which receives solutions to problems is to have the will of God absolutely clear. "And this is the confidence which we have in him, that if we ask anything according to his will he hears us. And if we know that he hears us in whatever we ask, we know that we have obtained the requests made of him" (1 John 5:14-15). If we ask according to His will, we already have the answer even as we pray and can therefore count upon seeing it. If I have found a word of God which makes clear His will concerning my particular problem, I can ask in full confidence that He heard and consequently I am receiving the answer even as I am praying.

Faith and Actions

Every step of faith must be followed by an act to manifest the inner faith. "Faith apart from works [actions] is dead" (James 2:26). In many of the Bible accounts of miracle faith, a definite action was required of those who were believing. For example, Moses was commanded to hold his staff over the Red Sea to open it. He struck the rock to obtain water. The Israelites had to look at the brazen serpent, to be healed. The ten lepers were to show themselves to the priest. The hemorrhaging woman touched Christ's garment. If you are trying to believe God for something, what action are you taking to manifest your faith? It may be a foolish act such as Naaman had to do to be cleansed of his leprosy. What you do is not so important as the faith that is made alive through the act. Often this act is simply the confessing with the lips the Word of God.

Faith and Words

The spoken word has power. Proverbs speaks of the tongue as having the power of life and death. Jesus taught, "Truly, I say to you, whoever *says* to this mountain, 'Be taken up and cast into the sea,' and does not doubt in his heart, but believes that what he *says* will come to pass, it will be done for him" (Mark 11:23). Often people claim to believe God but the confession of their mouth is continually negative and fatalistic. They incessantly overflow with problems. These people can never get free as long as they follow this practice. Whatever faith may be present in their hearts is made ineffective by their words: "For man believes with his heart and so is justified, and he confesses with his lips and so is saved" (Rom. 10:10).

A man is called right because of the inner faith but he is changed through the confession of his lips. That is, the outward manifestation of the inner life comes as confession to that life is made with the lips. The inner choice of the will must be exercised upon the Word of God, and then that choice must extend to the act of speaking aloud what the will has chosen. The Word of God must find its way to the lips. What a man has chosen to believe becomes established and concrete when he hears himself saying it. Whether or not another human hears him say it is incidental. The important thing is that God and the spirits, good and evil, and the man himself hear his testimony. It is easy to speak what we feel, but God wants us to speak what we have chosen to believe. This is the way to change the feelings. As the positive Word of God is declared, my feelings are being changed into that which I am speaking. On the other hand, if I declare my negative feelings, I will more and more feel like the feeling I already have. If I declare what God says over and against my feelings, those feelings will change to harmonize with the word I am believing and declaring.

The Psalmist prays, "Set a guard over my mouth, O Lord, keep watch over the door of my lips!" Do not allow your own words to destroy the faith of your heart. Speak that which God speaks. Your inward faith and outward word *must* be in unity. Do not allow the comfort of complaining about your circumstance when, at the same time, you are expecting God to change it. Instead, let your words be positive, in harmony with your expectations.

Faith and Patience

It may take some time until the answer to my prayer is manifested. In the meantime, I must by choice of my will count upon the clear promise or Word of God, and know the answer will become visible to me as Hebrews 11:1 declares. "Faith is the substance of things hoped for, the evidence of things not seen," or to paraphrase it, "Faith is the substance things hoped for are made of." It is possible that many of the things we pray for do not become manifest to us because we do not stay around to see the answer when it comes. It takes faith *and* patience to inherit the promise. The word patience here is used in the sense of *endurance.* I will not receive answers to my prayers unless I believe and *continue to believe.* This continuing to believe, the Bible calls patience or endurance: "For you have need of endurance, so that you may do the will of God and receive what is promised" (Heb. 10:36).

As we come to God with our needs in prayer, we must remember that His interests extend beyond the mere answering of a petition. We must not lose sight of the eternal purpose of God, which is the redemption of the world. In fulfilling this purpose He deals with each individual in a personal way by building a faith-trust relationship between the individual and Himself. God has already declared that His redemption is complete in fact, and a new creation was brought to reality and into existence in His Son. The hearer of this announcement must allow that word to operate in himself through trusting in the truthfulness of God and therefore counting upon God's declaration. In so doing, the word of God becomes life in the individual, and he receives the benefits of the truth, becoming a partaker of the new creation. Thus God's statement of fact becomes the individual's personal possession and experience. He is therefore in the process of redemption.

Faith is not a mere magic genii to produce things for me, but is God's way to reproduce His life in me. The adversities, needs, and problems that come into my life and drive me to God for help are His instruments to form Christ in my personality. These problems set in motion the process of faith. God desires Jesus Christ to be formed in my conscious life; therefore, the answer is often delayed and my faith tested. It is only in the testing of faith that God's redemptive purpose can bear fruit in my life, for if I react properly to the test I will depend upon the indwelling Christ to be my strength to endure. In this way, through trusting His life within me, Christ more and more is formed in my personality. James tells us the testing of faith produces endurance, and Paul, writing to the Romans, instructs us that endurance produces character. James puts it in these words, "For you know that the testing of your faith produces steadfastness. And let steadfastness have its full effect, that you may be perfect and complete, lacking in nothing" (James 1:3-4).

Yes, even in his apparent neglect of our

prayers, God reveals His love for us. He wants us to be perfect and complete, *lacking in nothing!* Therefore, "count it all joy, my brethren, when you meet various trials." Note that the apostle wrote "*count it all joy.*" This is a word of faith, for no trial ever *feels* good or joyful. He does not say *feel* joyful but *count* it all joy. We may have this positive faith because through it all our character is being changed into the glorious character and life of Jesus Christ. Faith which does not ultimately produce this new creation, either in myself or someone else, is purposeless and vain. God's primary purpose is to form Christ in the human being; therefore, the highest personal benefit from faith results when it is used in cooperation with God in accomplishing His high purpose.

All that I have written here is intended to add to your understanding of the Christian walk *after* you have had two experiences with God. The first, obviously, is to be born again. It would be ludicrous to speak of living a life before being born. Soul healing begins in the spirit, so the spirit must be made alive by receiving Jesus Christ. The second experience, while not as obvious as the first, is the baptism with the Holy Spirit. God loves you. He is working in you the abundant life and He desires your complete healing in body, soul and spirit. To insure this work, He has not left you to your own resources. Jesus died so that the Holy Spirit could be resident within you. He is your counselor, helper, comforter and guide to all the good things you have in Jesus. He will help you to apply the principles of faith and healing that I have tried to present to you in this booklet.

Jesus said, "These things I have spoken to you, while I am still with you. But the Counselor, the Holy Spirit, whom the Father will send in my name, he will teach you all things, and bring to your remembrance all that I have said to you" (John 14:25-26). "I have yet many things to say to you, but you cannot bear them now. When the Spirit of truth comes, he will guide you into all the truth; for he will not speak on his own authority, but whatever he hears he will speak, and he will declare to you the things that are to come. He will glorify me, for he will take what is mine and declare it to you. All that the Father has is mine; therefore I said that he will take what is mine and declare it to you" (John 16:12-15).

"Be filled with the Spirit, addressing one another in psalms and hymns and spiritual songs, singing and making melody to the Lord with all your heart." Trust Him. You cannot fail because God is on your side!

OTHER BOOKS
YOU MAY WANT TO READ

BEYOND PETITION
by Paris Reidhead
Six sensible steps into the heights of prayer, drawn from the teachings of the Epistles. Liberally spiced with illustrations from real-life people. 95¢

THE DISCIPLINED LIFE
by Richard Shelley Taylor
An unparalleled classic on the theme of the well-ordered Christian life. A clarion call to Godly discipline for the sake of maximum fruitfulness. $1.25

LIKE CHRIST
by Andrew Murray
Murray was obviously obsessed with Jesus. In 31 brief meditations he attempts to transmit that magnificent obsession to the reader. $1.45

THE RENEWED MIND (How To Be the Kind of Person You Want To Be)
by Larry Christenson
A series of chapters on specific ways of building character. Not simply a rehash of deeper-life themes, but an explanation of HOW to utilize the principles of the Christian life. The points are driven home by the use of parables and allegories. $2.45

Purchase these books at your local bookstore. If your bookstore does not have them, you may order from Bethany Fellowship, Inc., 6820 Auto Club Road, Minneapolis, Minnesota 55438. Enclose payment with your order, plus 10¢ per book for postage.